C000142524

Failure is hum[...]
The question i[...]
more importa[...]
partnership w[...]

The Bible does not shy away from the reality of human limitations and mistakes, from the story of Adam and Eve right through the struggles of the people of Israel in the time of Judges, through to Judas' betrayal and Peter's denials of Jesus. But the Christian story is ultimately a story of failings redeemed and of sins forgiven. Our journey through Lent will lead us to the seeming failure and humiliation of Jesus' death on the cross. It is through that seeming defeat, however, that we will ultimately come to the joy of Jesus' triumphant resurrection.

If we were to judge others – or ourselves – only by what we get wrong, there would not be much hope. But this year's *Dust and Glory* journey reminds us that the end of our story is written by God – and calls us to trust in God's merciful and hope-filled judgement.

Archbishop Justin Welby &
Archbishop Stephen Cottrell

ACKNOWLEDGEMENTS

Dust and Glory: A Lent journey of faith, failure and forgiveness **is the Church of England's theme for Lent 2023.**

These daily reflections are based on the Archbishop of Canterbury's 2023 Lent Book, *Failure: What Jesus said about sin, mistakes and messing stuff up* (SPCK) by Emma Ineson, Bishop to the Archbishops of Canterbury and York, recently announced as the next Bishop of Kensington.

The Church House Publishing and the Church of England Communications teams would like to express their gratitude to **SPCK Publishing** for their willingness to collaborate to maximise the range of print and digital resources offered to churches, discussion groups and individuals this year. And we are most grateful to Bishop Emma (and Abbie Martin who co-wrote the reflections with her) for ensuring close coordination between the Archbishops' Lent Book and the wider range of resources.

Details of the Lent book and the full range of resources to support this year's Lent theme can be found at CofE.io/DustAndGlory

CONTENTS

HOW TO USE THIS BOOKLET

Dust and Glory: A Lent journey of faith, failure and forgiveness **invites us to find God in the mess of everyday life.**

This booklet contains 40 reflections, one for each of the forty days in Lent, which begins on Ash Wednesday (which falls on 22 February 2023) and ends on Easter Eve (Saturday 8 April 2023), plus one for Easter Day. You can use it on its own, but my hope is that those who are also reading the Archbishop of Canterbury's Lent Book 2023, *Failure: What Jesus said about sin, mistakes and messing stuff up* (SPCK) either individually or as part of a discussion group will find it helpful, too.

For each week (starting on a Sunday from Week 1 onwards) there is:

- **A theme** which corresponds to the chapters of the 2023 Lent book
- **A brief introduction** to the theme and readings for the week
- **A simple prayer**.

Each week we explore the idea of failure from a different angle and explore the difference God's redeeming work in Jesus makes to how we deal with the challenges and shortcomings in our lives and our world.

For each day (Monday to Saturday) there are daily reflections which offer:

- **A theme**
- **A picture**
- **A short passage from the Bible**
- **A reflection** on the theme and reading
- **A challenge** linked to the day's theme.

Finally, there are a range of suggestions for **Going Further**.

There is also a version of the daily challenge for children (and their families) available in the accompanying booklet *Dust and Glory: A Lent journey for children*. This offers a weekly reading and prayer, together with a daily action to help all ages make sense of life's struggles and draw closer to God as we journey towards Easter.

The booklet will be accompanied by daily social media posts from Ash Wednesday to Easter Day, together with a wide range of video and other free digital resources for individuals, groups and churches available via **CofE.io/DustAndGlory**

Emma Ineson

A Mixture of Dust and Glory

Lent is traditionally a time when we acknowledge our failure to live up to God's purpose for our lives. And yet, in the shadow of the cross and the light of the resurrection, we find hope in the God who transforms failure into glory.

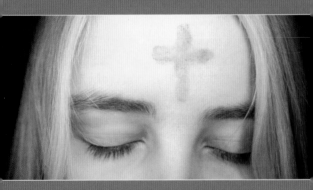

Prayer for the week

Lord Jesus, you spent forty days in the wilderness: walk with me in the wilderness of Lent and life. Hold my failures in the light of your compassion and guide me each day in your way. Amen.

Ash Wednesday
REMEMBER YOU ARE DUST

Read Genesis 3.19

> *By the sweat of your face you shall eat bread until you return to the ground, for out of it you were taken; you are dust, and to dust you shall return.*

Reflection

We begin Lent by looking back to the first book of the Bible, and the very first failure. We know the story: Adam and Eve disobey God and they eat the fruit that they have been told not to touch.

As a result, they are cast out of the Garden of Eden, condemned to suffering and death.

Fast forward to today, Ash Wednesday, the beginning of Lent. As the ash is placed on our foreheads in the shape of the cross, those words from Genesis are spoken: "Remember you are dust, and to dust you shall return." It is a day to lament our disconnectedness from God. It begins a time where we consider those failures in our own lives which separate us from God today.

But the sign of the cross reminds us that in Jesus, our failure is overcome by God's glory. God himself comes to make up the distance we put between him and us.

We all fail, in ways big or small, every day. That's part of being human.

Ask yourself honestly where you've stepped away from God recently.

DON'T BLAME ME!

Read Genesis 3.8-15

> " *The man said, "The woman whom you gave to be with me, she gave me fruit from the tree, and I ate." Then the Lord God said to the woman, "What is this that you have done?" The woman said, "The serpent tricked me, and I ate."* "

Reflection

Adam and Eve are too ashamed to admit their wrongs. Instead of taking responsibility, they seek to blame others. This is an easy trap to fall into, but it only ever makes things worse. Admitting you've got it wrong can be scary. No one likes to be judged or criticized or thought badly of by others. But we can't start to repair what has gone wrong until we're willing to admit it.

There is a tradition of "confession" in the Christian faith. Christians admit their sinfulness so they can start to dissolve some of the "stuff" that separates them from others and from God. They ask God's forgiveness and seek to make amends. Admitting we have done something bad can feel like a trap. But it is exactly when we place ourselves into God's hands we realise that his infinite mercy – his ability to transform any dead end into a turning point – is freedom.

Our church services regularly include "prayers of penitence," where we confess our sins. Try and look out for them this week (or look them up online) and reflect especially on that prayer.

Friday after Ash Wednesday
LIVING WITH FAILURE

Read Genesis 3.17-18

> *... cursed is the ground because of you; in toil you shall eat of it all the days of your life; thorns and thistles it shall bring forth for you; and you shall eat the plants of the field.*

Reflection

We all live with the consequences of failure. We fail to get jobs. We fail to be patient with our loved ones. We fail to do everything we say we're going to do in that flash of enthusiasm.

As individuals we might be aware of how we measure up against others, of relationships that have gone wrong, or of our bodies failing. On the news, we see failure on a global scale – conflict, famine, injustice, poverty.

Failure is the wallpaper of life. It hangs in the background, slowly building the scenery of our days. How can we live, surrounded as we are by failure? We can't shy away from it, or try and escape it, or live in constant fear of it. Otherwise, we'll live narrow lives, motivated by running away from failure rather than running towards full, exciting, hopeful lives.

So, failure. We'd better learn to live with it.

Think of an area of failure that you are living with. Is there a way you can live with it "better" – to be less afraid of it?

14

THE LONG ROAD FROM DUST TO GLORY

Read Genesis 3.20-24

> *The man named his wife Eve because she was the mother of all living.*

Reflection

We begin Lent by looking back at the first failure in the Bible. But the story doesn't end there. From Adam and Eve – two "failures" – spring countless more stories of failure and hope, relationships and life: stories that are made possible through the lives and legacies of other imperfect, flawed and fractured people.

Failure is inevitable, but isn't the end of the story.

All of us descendants of Eve live with failure. But throughout the Bible there is a persistent understanding that failure doesn't have the final word. From Noah to Moses, to Jacob, to David, God's grace means human failure doesn't prevent us from being part of God's people and doing God's work.

All of these characters in our Bibles we look up to and learn from today have their failures, yes. But they also become part of a much larger and longer story of God's people.

Think back to the area of failure you focused on yesterday. Try thinking of it in a wider context. How has – or might – it become part of the story of God and God's people?

What is Failure?

Books about failure tend to start by trying to define what it means. But even this is not straightforward. The word is a catch-all for all sorts of things that go wrong. We're quick to apply the title "failure" to others, and reluctant to admit it ourselves. So what is failure? That's what we will be exploring this week.

Prayer for the week

Lord, help me see clearly when things go wrong. May I not be swift to blame when others fail, and may I not run away when I myself fail. Amen.

GOOD FAILURE, BAD FAILURE

Read Jonah 3.3—4.5

> *Jonah prayed to the Lord and said, "O Lord! Is not this what I said while I was still in my own country? ... And now, O Lord, please take my life from me, for it is better for me to die than to live."*

Reflection

During the COVID pandemic, we got a bit of an insight into the blooper reel of other people's lives. From people being interrupted on zoom calls, forgetting they were only correctly dressed from the waist up, and the various connectivity issues ("You're on mute ... "), these mini-disasters actually brought us closer as we all muddled along together. Failure can be endearing. Seeing other people as vulnerable and human too can be quite comforting. Jonah's failure is quite endearing and funny. At first he tries haplessly to run away. Then when the people of Nineveh listen to his warning and change their ways, he stomps around the city, throws a strop at God for being merciful to them and goes off to sulk under a tree.

But other failures have the opposite effect. When a politician has lied or when someone says something hurtful on social media, we feel angry. Different types of failure elicit very different responses.

What failures in others do you find funny or endearing? And what failures do you find offensive and dangerous? Why do you think that is?

WHAT IS A FAILURE ANYWAY?

Read Mark 14.66-72

> *But Peter denied it, saying, "I do not know or understand what you are talking about." And he went out into the forecourt. And a cock crowed.*

Reflection

Perhaps the worst thing is to be a "failure". To wear it as a garment that can't be taken off, to have this label at the heart of your identity feels so final.

That's how many of us respond when things go wrong. We leapfrog over "I have failed" straight to "I am a failure."

People are, of course, so much more nuanced than that. We are much more than one action, or one thought, or one sentence. We are a complicated muddle of doing well, doing badly and being somewhere in the middle of the flux.

Take Peter, for example. Peter failed on a huge scale. He denied Jesus three times, after totally denying that he would deny him! And yet that same Peter – cowardly, dishonest Peter – became one of the great pillars of the Church. Was he a failure? Yes, and no. More importantly, he was forgiven, and loved, and defined by God.

Make a list of the things you think define you – builder, nurse, artist, son, mother, carer, runner, singer, etc.

How do you think God defines you?

RISKING FAILURE

Read Genesis 12.1-4

> *Now the Lord said to Abram, "Go from your country and from your kindred and your father's house to the land that I will show you ..." So Abram went, as the Lord has told him ...*

Reflection

Sometimes – whisper it – failure is actually A Very Good Thing. It means we have taken a chance to try something new, that we've been bold and taken risks.

And sometimes we have to take the right risks for the right reasons, otherwise we would never move forward, learn new things or develop new relationships. Maybe we won't get it right the first time – or the first hundred times – but each time, we will be a little closer.

Abraham takes big risks in leaving his country, his people and his homeland. And he makes plenty of mistakes as well. God doesn't expect us to be perfect on the journey, he just wants us to go with him.

Sometimes trying things that might fail is to be encouraged.

How can you put this into practice in your own life?

Thursday, Week 1
THE FEAR FACTOR

Read Psalm 56.1-4

> *O Most High, when I am afraid, I put my trust in you. In God, whose word I praise, in God I trust; I am not afraid ...*

Reflection

The main thing that stops us from trying new things is the fear of getting it wrong. We worry that we'll be found inadequate, or we'll be embarrassed.

A healthy amount of fear is a good thing, but sometimes fear of failure is crippling. At its heart is a fear of shame: the belief that we are flawed and unworthy of love, belonging and connection.

That need for self-protection to avoid shame is why we often don't admit what we've got wrong. The worry is that we learn to live lives that are fearful rather than faithful – smaller, rather than expansive, turned in to ourselves rather than out to the world.

God leads us out of fear and into faith. Through faith we are able to try new things, take bold steps and know that it is the attempt, not the outcome, that matters.

What is something you've been avoiding out of fear of failure?

Can you take a step towards it today?

Friday, Week 1

IMPERFECT SAINTS
(AND PERFECT SINNERS)

Read Mark 10.35–45

> *But Jesus said to them, "You do not know what you are asking. Are you able to drink the cup that I drink or be baptized with the baptism that I am baptized with?"*

Reflection

The funny thing is that Christians ought to be really good at failure. Jesus constantly made it clear to his disciples that following him, despite their hopes, wasn't an instant route to worldly success. It would, in all likelihood, lead to their deaths.

When the disciples argued over who was the most important and would sit in the best place in heaven, Jesus was clear with them that their expectations were sure to be disappointed – or at least fulfilled in a way they definitely didn't expect.

Jesus prepares us for failure as well. He calls us to take up our cross and follow him. Life as a Christian is many wonderful things, but it is not easy. We are called to step into the suffering and mess of the world, just as Jesus did, not to avoid it.

It is on this difficult path that we are offered life in all its fullness.

How do we respond when life is difficult? Do we feel surprised or angry? Or do we accept Jesus' invitation to walk the tough path he has trodden?

APPEARANCES CAN BE DECEIVING

Read Matthew 27.33–44

> *You who would destroy the temple and build it in three days, save yourself! If you are the Son of God, come down from the cross?*

Reflection

It's easy to forget what a shameful failure the cross seemed to be. After Easter, we cast it in the warm glow of the resurrection. But Lent is a time to remember how the crucifixion was a symbol of the ultimate shame and failure. The fact that Jesus is led to his death wearing a crown of thorns and a purple robe – ironic success symbols – underlines how badly Jesus had failed in the eyes of those who condemned him. And yet it's through this icon of foolishness and failure that God chose to shame the apparent wisdom of the world (1 Corinthians 1.27).

Appearances can be deceiving. Sometimes what seems obvious to us isn't the whole story. Maybe we've misunderstood it, maybe our own experiences have coloured our perspective of it, maybe we've made assumptions based on our own hopes or fears. What looks like failure and weakness might just be the strength that only comes from vulnerability.

There are many things that society thinks look like weakness that might actually be strength. Stepping away from a difficult situation, deciding to let go of pursuing a goal. Is there something like this in your life?

Understanding Sin

The Christian faith teaches that all human beings are sinful. When we're thinking about what it means to fail, that's a surprisingly comforting thought. Rather than idolizing people and waiting for them to fall off a pedestal, Christian faith encourages us to start from a low point, and work up.

Prayer for the week

Lord, I know I am a sinner. I rejoice that you sent your only Son to die for my sins, that I might be redeemed and saved by your love. Amen.

COME BACK SIN, ALL IS FORGIVEN?

Read Romans 3.21-26

> ... *all have sinned and fall short of the glory of God.*

Reflection

Sin is a word and concept that has found its way into popular culture. But instead of referring to the utter depravity of the human condition, it's associated with eating something you really shouldn't, or telling a little fib. It's come to be a word you use in quotation marks with a wink, a fun little phrase that indicates something is naughty but nice.

What happened to sin?

Sin, for Christians, is really about separation from God. It's about those choices we make and temptations we fall victim to that are contrary to what God wants for us.

Sin is really about ruptured relationships – with God, with one another, with ourselves. Between individuals and communities, in ways small and big, sin is what keeps us isolated, hopeless and suffering.

There are relationships in all of our lives that aren't as we wish they would be.

Today, try praying for God to bring healing to those relationships.

WHO INVENTED SIN?

Read Genesis 2.15-17

> *… but you must not eat from the tree of the knowledge of good and evil, for when you eat from it you will certainly die.*

Reflection

The question of when and how sin first entered into the human experience is one that has long preoccupied theologians and philosophers.

Was the introduction of sin into the Garden of

Eden the fault of Adam who ate the apple? Or
Eve who gave it to him? Or God who gave them
free will? Or the serpent who persuaded them? Or
again God, who created the serpent?

To ask where sin originated is to fall into the trap
of thinking of all sin as "someone's fault" which
isn't really the point. When relationships are
fractured, there are almost always many reasons
why. Relationships are multi-faceted – including
our relationship with God.

When we think about whether people are totally
good or totally bad, it might be tempting to put
people into one category or the other, depending
on whether or not we like them. The challenge
is to see the dividing line between good and evil
not between people, but within each person.

Is there a situation in your life you have been
seeking to blame someone else for? What
might their perspective be?

ORIGINAL SIN

Read Psalm 51.1-5

> *For I know my transgressions, and my sin is ever before me... Indeed, I was born guilty, a sinner when my mother conceived me.*

Reflection

Original sin is the belief that sin isn't just something we do; it is something we are. We are sinners who do sinful things because we are sinners. St Augustine believed that everyone

is a sinner from the moment they are born –
imagine sin being like a part of our DNA,
a fundamental piece of who we are.

So naturally, the question we might ask is this:
What does it mean for us, as individuals, if we
are part of a system infected with sin at its very
core? How can we escape it?

There is some good news to this puzzling
conundrum. Even though sin has corrupted all
people for all time, as the view goes, so also
the grace and redemption of Christ is available
for all people for all time. As Paul writes to the
Corinthians, "for as all die in Adam, so all will be
made alive in Christ" (1 Corinthians 15.22).

**Spend some time reading and praying
through Psalm 51 today.**

CORPORATE SIN

Read Romans 5.12-17

> *Therefore, just as sin came into the world through one man, and death came through sin, and so death spread to all because all have sinned.*

Reflection

One of the things that we learned during the pandemic is that we don't exist in isolation from each other (despite the need sometimes to self-isolate). Our individual actions have an effect on others.

Scientific evidence showed that the wearing of masks during a pandemic, for example, is more likely to protect others from catching COVID from you than it is to stop you catching it from them. The pandemic taught us that it is not possible to be an island. All our actions and intentions are interrelated and interdependent.

So it is with sin. We take individual responsibility for our own sins and yet we are part of a system, a world in which sinfulness is inherent and we can never fully escape from it or its effects. What we can do is treat others with the compassion and forgiveness with which we wish to be treated, and love our neighbour as Jesus calls us to.

All the things you do affect other people – directly or indirectly.

What's one thing you could change that might help someone else today?

I SIN, YOU SIN, WE ALL SIN

Read Romans 5.18-21

> *For just as by the one man's disobedience the many were made sinners, so by the one man's obedience the many will be made righteous.*

Reflection

If we understand creation as being in a fallen state then individual human beings are part and parcel of that fallenness.

So does that mean we don't have to take individual responsibility for the things we do wrong? Are people a result of the badness that is in the world, in societies and in individual people's circumstances? How much personal responsibility do we need take for our failings?

The Bible would find the question about whether sin is corporate or individual rather an odd question. The two are closely linked. Paul, writing to the Romans, makes the link between the sin of the one Adam and the sin of the many. Likewise the beneficial effects of the redemption brought about by one man (Jesus) spreads to the many (all Christians).

Our own actions are influenced by many factors – and the consequences of those actions go far beyond affecting only ourselves.

Sometimes, things aren't our fault, but they are our responsibility. Can you think of a situation like that in your life?

40

HOPE FOR ALL SINNERS

Read Romans 5.1-11

> *God proves his love for us in that while we still were sinners Christ died for us.*

Reflection

We have looked a lot at sin this week. That's because, unless we understand a bit more about sin, we can't really get to the heart of what it means to fail and to get up again, and what it means to be human being who learns from their mistakes.

This is the perspective that sin gives us that we need most. If all human beings are totally sinful and there is no hope of redemption then we may as well give up now and let the world go to hell in a handcart.

But if God somehow entered our world to deal with our sins, to deal with our sinfulness and our failings and our fallen human nature, and died to make it possible to redeem it, then there is hope. God has given us this hope in Christ, as Paul writes in our reading today: 'and hope does not disappoint us'.

Take time today to simply reflect on God's goodness. Let our failures make us aware of our need for God.

Sinning as Well as We Can?

Last week we spent a lot of time thinking about the nature, origins and consequences of sin. We discovered that sin is an inevitable part of life. So, given that none of us can be perfect, how can we at least sin as well as we possibly can?

Prayer for the week

Lord, be with me in all the hard moments of this week, help me face up to my sin in the certainty that you love me beyond measure. Amen.

ADMIT YOU ARE "QUITE A SINNER"

Read Luke 18.9-14

> *But the tax-collector, standing far off, would not even look up to heaven, but was beating his breast and saying, "O God, be merciful to me, a sinner."*

Reflection

If we see sin as the ultimate failure, then admitting that we're all sinners is not a bad place to start in coming to terms with how to live well with failure. Indeed, it may be a liberation.

To admit that we commit sins, that we are part of a sinful humanity, that we are all sinners, is to join in what Dietrich Bonhoeffer called "the fellowship of the undevout": those who are so aware of their own failure and need of redemption that there is no need for pretence. The mercy and grace of God take centre stage.

Admitting "Yes, I am quite a sinner" (to quote Martin Luther) comes as liberation not condemnation. Once we acknowledge and accept that we are sinful human beings, we can let go of our exhausting attempts to redeem ourselves or to earn our way into heaven by our own efforts.

Have a go today at praying The Jesus Prayer – which draws on the words of the tax-collector in our reading today:

"Lord Jesus Christ, Son of God, have mercy on me, a sinner."

GET INTO TRAINING

Read Hebrews 5.11-14

> *But solid food is for the mature, those whose faculties have been trained by practice to distinguish good from evil.*

Reflection

Although we are indeed sinners, we are sinners beloved of God. Within us dwells God's Holy Spirit, whose job it is (among other things) daily to make us more like Jesus – or become less sinful.

This is the process of sanctification, or "becoming more holy". Sanctification is the ongoing movement – once a person has recognized that they are a sinner and have begun to repent – of the Christian heart towards a greater love of God and more closely living in the ways of God's kingdom.

And how to do that? The answer is slightly surprising and maybe not a little unpopular in today's fast-track, short-cut world where we can have anything we want, wherever we want it, immediately. The answer is in what we do with our habits.

So what we need to do is train our desires to be more in tune with the heart of God and his kingdom.

Habits are such an important part of our spiritual discipline. What is one habit you can begin or renew today to be more in tune with the heart of God?

OUR SINS ARE NOT SMALL

Read 2 Samuel 12.1-7a

> *Then David's anger was greatly kindled against the man. He said to Nathan, "As the Lord lives, the man who has done this deserves to die ... because he did this thing , and because he had no pity." Nathan said to David, "You are the man!"*

Reflection

One of the greatest deficiencies of the human condition is that we imagine that our sins are small. The cognitive dissonance we experience daily – "I am a good person, I deserve more, I am worth it; so why do I keep doing and saying and thinking bad things and why do bad things keep happening to me?" – comes about because we tend to say we have no sin and so "the truth is not in us" (1 John 1.8).

Sin? Me? No, surely not! But minimizing our own sinfulness has three consequences. First, when we do sin big we're shocked and feel even more like failures. Second, it leads us to be more judgemental of others, as David is in our reading today. Finally, it means we tend to excuse ourselves from the part we play in the sinfulness of humanity as a whole. Each of us needs to own our own part in the "big sins" of the world.

There are so many big problems in the world that go far beyond one person – poverty, injustice, conflict. If you are honest with yourself, are there small things you do to contribute to big problems?

OUR PART IN THE WORLD'S "BIG SINS"

Read Matthew 5.21-26

❝ *You have heard that it was said to those of ancient times, 'You shall not murder'; and 'whoever murders shall be liable to judgement'. But I say to you that if you are angry with a brother or sister, you will be liable to judgement …* ❞

Reflection

Sin is both a power and a behaviour. We don't need – nor are we able to – choose between the two or prioritise one over the other.

Perhaps the most obvious example of this is the way the sin of racism has historically shaped and continues to shape the way our world, particularly in the West, is ordered. One of the revelations of recent thinking on racism is that it is not enough simply to be not racist myself. I must also acknowledge the fact that I am shaped by a history and a society where I have benefitted because of a history of colonialism, racism and oppression.

What is my responsibility in relation to this kind of structural or systemic sin?

The first step is awareness. Second, there is a need to listen and understand. Thirdly, there is a need to speak out about what we now know is wrong and sinful.

Think of a big injustice that is part of society. How might you follow the three-step process of awareness, understanding and speaking out about it?

51

FORGETTING LIKE GOD FORGETS PART 1

Read Isaiah 43.16-25

> *Thus says the Lord: I, I am He who blots out your transgressions for my own sake, and I will not remember your sins.*

Reflection

"If we confess our sins," St John writes, "he who is faithful and just will forgive us our sins and cleanse us from all unrighteousness" (1 John 1.9). Yes, God calls us to own up to – or confess – our sins. But once this confession has taken place, God does something remarkable with our sins, and his memory of them. In fact the Bible shows us a God who is so ready and willing to forgive sins that he can't even remember them half the time: "I will not remember your sins," God says in our reading from Isaiah today.

God might be perfect, but he's very forgetful when it comes to our sin, negligent, even, in not counting our sins against us. That is a great encouragement to all of us who consider ourselves failures. With the awakening to the knowledge of sin comes inevitable guilt, but even as that happens God has already provided the solution, and has blotted out our sin.

You might be holding on to something you did wrong in the past. Perhaps it still has a big hold on you. Ask the God who is ready to forget your wrong to help you forgive yourself today.

FORGETTING LIKE GOD FORGETS PART 2

Read Romans 4.6-8

> *Blessed are those whose iniquities are forgiven, and whose sins are covered ...*

Reflection

Now we know that God doesn't just forgive our sins but forgets them, how does that help us deal with those who may have done us a great wrong – perhaps an unforgiveable wrong?

Telling people to "forgive" others has sometimes been a continuation of the wrong that has been done to them, a denial of its severity and an avoidance of proper justice. We have seen it happen to victims of abuse, communities who have been terribly treated, to women and children harmed in relationships, and many other vulnerable groups.

Forgiveness is vitally important, but equally important is understanding power dynamics in relationships and systems, recognising that forgiveness is the victims' choice alone and that forgiveness will often come alongside repentance, consequences and justice. There may well be certain things we find too difficult to forgive. All we can do is hand them over to the God who judges everyone with perfect justice and mercy.

Meditate on this line from the Lord's Prayer today: *"Forgive us our sins as we forgive those who sin against us."* How might you put this into practice?

Failure and the Church

Hopefully the idea of "the Church" brings many good things to mind for you – love, worship, community. But perhaps there are some things that annoy you too – division, failures and frustrations with the institution. This week we consider what it means for us to be part of a Church that is made up of human beings, and as such is prone to failure.

Prayer for the week

Lord, we thank you that you love your Church, the Body of Christ. Help us be the sign of your love for the whole world. Amen.

WHAT'S SO IMPORTANT ABOUT THE CHURCH?

Read Ephesians 3.7-13

> *... so that through the church the wisdom of God in its rich variety might now be made known to the rulers and authorities in the heavenly places.*

Reflection

Paul's vision in Ephesians is that "church" isn't an optional extra we can add on to a personal faith in Jesus if we feel like it. Membership of the Body of Christ, with our siblings, this radical new inclusive community of belonging and reconciliation, is absolutely central to the gospel.

When we're talking about "the Church" in Ephesians, we are talking the gathering of all God's people, called out and saved throughout all time and history to gather around the throne of Jesus, the heavenly assembly, the universal, cosmic, multi-national, multi-racial, boundary-less community of saved and reconciled people.

And through this assembly of "called out" ones, the manifold wisdom of God will be made known. The "wisdom" of God is his wonderful redemption plan to unite heaven and earth, and all peoples, through the death of his Son Jesus on the cross.

Whether we like it or not, we're not just individual Christians. We are part of a new community of God's people. What do you think that community should look like?

Tuesday, Week 4
RELATIONAL SINS

Read Galatians 5.16-26

> *Now the works of the flesh are obvious: sexual immorality, impurity, debauchery, idolatry, sorcery, enmities, strife, jealousy, anger, quarrels, dissensions, factions, envy, drunkenness, carousing, and things like these.*

Reflection

This passage in Galatians is a difficult one for us, and it often feels easier to ignore it. When we do, rarely, look at it, we often seem to focus on the "juicy" sins – "sexual immorality, impurity, debauchery, idolatry, sorcery ... drunkenness, carousing". We often forget or overlook the more boring relational sins: "enmities, strife, jealousy, anger, quarrels, dissensions, factions, envy".

And yet how often do we see these particular "works of the flesh" consuming churches and communities, as people fall out with each other, fail to love each other, and descend into factions and parties (and not the fun kind)?

These sins of "communal discord" which Paul lists in Galatians 5 are very much evident in both the Church and the wider world. But what marks the Church out as different – as God's Church – is our willingness to love those with whom we differ, disagree and whom perhaps we even dislike.

Where there are communities, there is often discord. Think for a moment about a Christian community you are part of. Do any of the sins Paul talks about in Galatians seem to be present?

POWERS AND PRINCIPALITIES

Read Ephesians 6.10-20

" *For our struggle is not against blood and flesh but against the rulers, against the authorities, against the cosmic powers of this present darkness, against the spiritual forces of evil in the heavenly places.* "

Reflection

The ways of God's kingdom are not the ways of the world. Jesus himself made that clear: "My kingdom is not of this world" (John 18.36).

The kingdom of God – that overarching framework in which Jesus understood his mission and in which we continue to view the work of the church – sets itself over against the "kingdoms" (and powers and principalities) who occupy this world in "this present darkness".

We are citizens of another kingdom, living in a land under occupation, and that demands a different approach. Jesus taught the disciples to operate in a way that subverted the powers and principalities of the world by giving them signposts, telling them stories about God's kingdom. And he left space for them to fail in pursuit of it.

Think about power in our world – who has it and how we perceive it – and the power Jesus showed us in the Gospels. How do they differ?

WHAT DO WE DO WITH THE PAST?

Read Matthew 5.23-24

> "So when you are offering your gift at the altar, if you remember that your brother or sister has something against you, leave your gift there before the altar and go; first be reconciled to your brother or sister, and then come and offer your gift."

Reflection

One of ways the Church has failed is in events in its history, with resonances in the present, where things went very badly wrong. In recent years the Church of England has made commitments to address the historic wrongs perpetrated by the church in the past – and to stop those things happening again.

So what to do with these failures of the past? How can a church – or indeed any institution – today meaningfully apologise on behalf of people from long ago? What form should repentance and justice take?

We can't change history, but we can become aware of damaging things that happened in the past and commit to put right their effects in the present. Although turning back the clock is impossible, we need to do the next best thing – to say sorry and to do all that can be done to put it right.

None of us can undo our actions. But it is never too late to apologize. Is there something in your past (however long ago) that you can apologize for?

Friday, Week 4

DIVISION IS NOT THE ANSWER

Read John 17.20-24

> *I ask ... that they may all be one. As you, Father, are in me and I am in you, may they also be in us, so that the world may believe that you have sent me.*

Reflection

In Monday's reading, we heard Paul telling the Ephesians that the Church is the means by which God shows to the hidden forces of this world the wisdom of God's plan to reconcile all people to himself through the cross of Christ. The mere existence of the Church demonstrates that Christ has been victorious.

The way you prove that something was a wise plan is to show it working.

So when the Church demonstrates its unity, when the Church rises up to be all the Church it can be, bringing reconciliation, challenging injustice, heralding freedom, proclaiming good news; when we refuse hostility and division, when we treat each other – everyone – as Christian brothers and sisters, then we show to the rulers and authorities the wisdom of God, by being the Church Christ died to create.

Jesus calls us to unity, even (maybe especially) with those who are different from us.

Can you find something you have in common with someone who is very different to you today?

HOW WE ARE, NOT JUST WHO WE ARE

Credit: Diocese of Birmingham

Read Revelation 2.1-7

> *... you have abandoned the love you had at first.*

Reflection

There is no ideal Church, only the one that exists. So how do we reconcile this amazing, cosmic vision of who and what the Church is with the limited, fractured and fallible organization we see enacted in our pews and parsonages, and in the pages of our news outlets day after day?

We need to focus less on what we are, and the limits and boundaries of that, less on what we do, and the way our own efforts might save us, and more on the way we are together, the quality of our being and our relating – how we are church.

In the words of Revelation, we need as a church to rekindle the love we had at first. Let's be kind to each other, and focus more on the qualities that have the potential to bring us together, not drive us apart. For in the end we are, together, a demonstration of the wisdom God, no more and no less.

How do we treat others, particularly when we disagree? Is it with kindness, openness and compassion, or do we try and preserve our own interests? Bear that in mind today.

Living Well with Failure

Over the past four weeks' reflections we have looked failure full in the face. We've accepted it, examined it – perhaps even embraced it. This week we will now explore how to live well as a failure in the here and now.

Prayer for the week

Lord, you are strong when we are frail, and gentle when we let you down. Help us to lean on you this week. Amen.

LIVING IN THE MESS

Read Psalm 107.1-9

> *Some wandered in desert wastes, finding no way to an inhabited town … their soul fainted within them. Then they cried out to the Lord in their trouble …*

Reflection

When I procrastinate, I tidy. I organize each room, I fold the sheets, I tidy the drawers and get the laundry in order. It's so beautiful. The trouble is that I tend to try to do with life what I have just done with my house – that is, get it all tidy and in order. And that's not possible. We do what we can to make things better, but it's equally important to learn to live in the mess that's an inevitable consequence of living.

So what can we learn about ourselves through living in the mess? One of the things we note is that God is closer to the mess than we might imagine, and our messy lives and world are never out of the scope of God's love and redemption. Indeed "mess" might even be part of God's plan. He is always present with us in it.

Whether we're facing physical mess, emotional mess, financial mess or any other kind – do we shut God out of it, or do we "cry out to the Lord in our trouble" to step into the confusion of our lives?

FAILING WIDELY

Read John 21.1-11

> *They went out and got into the boat, but that night they caught nothing. Just after daybreak, Jesus stood on the beach ... He said to them, "Cast the net to the right side of the boat, and you shall find some."*

Reflection

Jesus set the disciples on the right path when they were failing at their task. I have learned from many different kinds of mistakes. It doesn't mean I won't make mistakes again – it means I won't make those particular mistakes again.

One of the things most often said is that failure presents an opportunity to learn and to do things differently. But it's not that easy is it? Sometimes we fail to learn from our mistakes. We make the same ones again and again.

Learning from failure is different to turning failure into success. In learning from failure, you may simply be learning not to mess things up so badly, or in the same way, next time.

Learning from our failures may actually be about making life a little more tolerable, not incredibly successful. Perhaps we need to set the bar quite low when it comes to learning from failure?

Think of a mistake you have made this week, whether small or large. What can you learn from it? What can you do to try to ensure it doesn't happen again?

Wednesday, Week 5
"KNOW THYSELF"

Read Hebrews 12.1-2

> *Therefore, since we are surrounded by so great a cloud of witnesses, let us also lay aside every weight and the sin that clings so closely, and let us run with perseverance the race that is set before us …*

Reflection

The way to be a person who fails really well is to be self-aware about the ways in which you are most likely to fail and the things that are most likely to cause you to do so. And to work with others towards owning both, speaking with kindness for yourself about it when it happens.

Knowing what these flaws are, and being aware of how they impact our interactions, is half the battle. Where they are unacknowledged, they are at their most powerful. And a lack of self-awareness is what is most likely to cause us to fail and make mistakes.

Accepting the fact that mistakes were made, and allowing and acknowledging the feelings that raises in us with grief and compassion rather than denial, anger and rage, mean we are able to learn from our failings and turn that learning into wisdom.

Think honestly to yourself about where you're likely to fail. Are you forgetful, or do you become easily angry? Try to call these things to mind without judgement, just an awareness that means they are easier to spot, and so handle.

ALLOWING OTHERS TO FAIL

Read: Hebrews 13.5-8

> *Remember your leaders, those who spoke the word of God to you; consider the outcome of their way of life, and imitate their faith.*

Reflection

The antidote to the shame that is invariably experienced around failure is to get it out into the open. C. S. Lewis spoke about friendship being born the moment one person says to another,

"What? You too? I thought I was the only one."

Being aware of our own failures means we are more likely in turn to be forgiving of the failures of others. Sharing our failures is not easy and there aren't many safe places in which to do so. But if there were more, we might be happier people within healthier communities and organizations, more like the "leaders" in our reading today.

One of the benefits of sharing our failures is that it in turn gives permission for others to do likewise. Sharing failures gives others permission to fail also and be open about it in order to learn. Imagine what life would look like if we truly allowed others to fail, just as we do.

We've talked about how it's scary to admit our failures, but perhaps it is one of the habits we can build. How can you build relationships where sharing failures, as well as successes, is normal?

HOW TO
BE WRONG

Read: 1 Kings 19.7-12

> *Then the word of the Lord came to him, saying, "What are you doing here, Elijah?" He answered, "I have been very zealous for the Lord ... I alone am left, and they are seeking my life, to take it away."*

Reflection

One of the skills we need most to learn in living well with failure is how to be wrong. The realization that you might be wrong about something happens most often after you've had an argument with someone else about it. Elijah, in today's reading, is certain he has been forsaken by God, and feels betrayed and angry.

The world seems to be a very angry place at present, which is perhaps not surprising when you consider what we're up against. However, one of the skills that it would be really good for Christians to develop, is to get better at seeing the complexities and nuances of an argument and at learning to really listen well to the perspectives of those with whom we disagree.

The highest compliment from someone who disagrees with you is not "You were right," it's "You made me think."

Having arguments is sometimes healthy! It's not normal to agree all the time. But when we argue, can we change the goal from "winning" to "learning"?

79

Weekend, Week 5
FAILURE IS NEVER FINAL

Read: John 8.1-11

> **"***Neither do I condemn you. Go your way, and from now on do not sin again.***"**

Reflection

Jesus does not condemn the woman the crowd condemns. He sees her, loves her, and sets her free.

God looks at us differently to the way we see ourselves (and the way society sees us), and we're in very good company – along with Abraham, Moses and Joseph – as those who have failed but whom God is able to use in his purposes.

It is our faith in God's hopeful future in Christ that defines us, not our failures. We are not defined by our failures any more than we're defined by our successes.

When things are broken through failure the answer is not to throw them out with the rubbish, but to work on repairing them, restoring them. We've all messed up. We're broken. We have got things wrong and damaged ourselves and others. But what if God's promise was to take all that and slowly, carefully, painstakingly, with our help and cooperation, put things right again?

Can you think of someone you or society has been condemning recently? How might Jesus react?

81

The Greatest Failure of all?

Holy Week sounds like the story of the greatest failure of all. A man who rode into a city as a king, applauded, revered and welcomed on Sunday is abandoned and hanging from a cross by Friday. And yet ultimately, this "failure" will prove to be God's greatest victory.

Challenge for the week

Try to make time each day during this Holy Week for prayer, reflecting on the story at the heart of our faith.

Lord Jesus, you came to Jerusalem in triumph, only to be shunned, abused, rejected and betrayed. Help us know the difference between our ideas of victory and your eternal, triumphant, and righteous glory. Amen.

THE EXPECTATIONS OF THE CROWD

Read Matthew 21.1-11

> *Hosanna to the Son of David! Blessed is the one who comes in the name of the Lord! Hosanna in the highest heaven!*

Reflection

Palm Sunday is a day of triumph. The crowds welcome Jesus to Jerusalem. They shout accolades, they wave palm branches to welcome him. They place in him a longstanding hope –

that this will be a king that will liberate them from Roman rule, re-establish them as God's chosen people and – as the descendent of King David – return them to power and might.

Reality sets in very quickly. It becomes clear that Jesus is not going to wage war, to lead an army against the Romans or stage the sort of uprising they had anticipated would result in victory. Instead, Jesus spends time with the outcasts. He tells stories about a very different kingdom. He predicts his own death at the hands of those he was supposed to conquer.

People's expectations of a mighty king are deflated. He is betrayed by his friends. What happens when we don't fulfil others' expectations of us, or even our expectations of ourselves?

Lord Jesus, help us not to seek the adoration of the crowd, but your righteousness. Help us not to pursue domination, but service. Help us not to seek our power, but your kingdom. Amen.

Tuesday of Holy Week
SETTING US UP TO FAIL?

Read Mark 13.9-13

> *As for yourselves, beware; for they will hand you over to councils; and you will be beaten ... and you will be hated by all because of my name.*

Reflection

There are many blogs, courses, and opinions on how to lead nowadays. Most of them espouse a sort of motivational, encouraging leadership – a leadership oriented towards success and profit.

That's not the sort of leader Jesus was. Throughout Holy Week, Jesus seems to train his disciples for failure. He knew the path to which he called them was more likely to earn them suffering than success, grief than glory.

He sent them out in the sure knowledge that they would encounter rejection more often than recognition. And, of course, the disciples failed an awful lot. They misunderstood, they argued, they jockeyed for position.

So Jesus was used to dealing with failure in others. He anticipated the failure of his disciples, trained them for it even, and was merciful when he encountered failure in others, always giving a second chance.

Lord Jesus, prepare us for failure as you prepared your disciples. Be merciful where we do fail, forgive us where we misunderstand, and give us the cup you drink. Amen.

JESUS HAS TIME FOR "FAILURES"

Read Matthew 21.28-32

> *Jesus said to them, "Truly I tell you, the tax collectors and the prostitutes are going into the kingdom of God ahead of you!"*

Reflection

It wasn't just the disciples who failed. Jesus spent a lot of time with the people society deemed to be failures in some way. From Zacchaeus to the woman caught in adultery, Jesus sought out, welcomed and accepted those whom others condemned. He pointed out that those who judged others harshly were likely forgetting their own failures.

Jesus didn't wait for failed people to become respectable or successful before he welcomed them into the kingdom. And of course, this is what really angered the religious leaders and occupying forces – by claiming to forgive sins and putting himself on a par with God (which was kind of the point), Jesus had broken down a social order that privileged some and penalized others, and offered instead a new community in which everyone, especially the flawed and fractured, were still beloved by God.

Lord Jesus, you sought out and loved those society shunned and called unlovable. Help us to do the same: not to associate ourselves with power and popularity, but to be close to those you are close to. Amen.

Maundy Thursday
PREPARING TO FAIL

Read Matthew 26.20-25

When it was evening, he took his place with the twelve; and while they were eating, he said, "Truly I tell you, one of you will betray me."

Reflection

"Failing to prepare is preparing to fail," as the old saying goes. At the Last Supper, we quite literally see Jesus, knowing he is close to death, preparing to "fail", and preparing his friends for it as well.

Maundy Thursday is a day packed full of failure. The disciples fail to understand what Jesus is doing when he washes their feet, and they fail to stay awake in Gethsemane. Judas fails Jesus when he betrays him to the authorities. Peter fails Jesus when he denies knowing him three times.

What is amazing is that Jesus still goes to the cross for this group, people who have betrayed him, denied him, misunderstood him, and failed him.

Jesus doesn't die for perfect people who love God perfectly and have no need of forgiveness. He dies for us when we are sinners, when we reject him, when we ignore him, and when we deny him.

Lord Jesus, you died for us while we were still your enemies. May we, too, be willing to love those who hurt us, make sacrifices for those who let us down and forgive those who betray us. Amen.

Good Friday
THE "FAILURE" OF THE CROSS?

Read Matthew 27.38-46

> *From noon on, darkness came over the whole land until three in the afternoon. And about three o'clock Jesus cried with a loud voice, "Eli, Eli, lema sabachthani?' that is, 'My God, my God, why have you forsaken me?' "*

Reflection

I am in no doubt that the cross felt like failure to Jesus. That's why he cried out "My God, my God why have you forsaken me?" In this way we can say that Jesus experienced failure as we do. He experienced desolation.

And yet the cross was very much not failure. If failure is when something doesn't go to plan, the cross was not failure because the cross was God's plan all along. Jesus knew that and taught his disciples as much: "The Son of Man must undergo great suffering, and be rejected by the elders, chief priests, and scribes, and be killed, and on the third day be raised" (Luke 9.22).

What felt like failure to Jesus was not the lack of things progressing according to the plan, but his experience of complete separation from God – being forsaken.

Lord Jesus, on the cross, you knew separation from your Father so that we might never be separated from God again. In our desolation and isolation may we know your presence with us always. Amen.

Easter Eve
THE LONGEST SATURDAY

Read John 16.16-17

> A little while, and you will no longer see me, and again a little while, and you will see me.

Reflection

There was a day where no one knew whether the cross was "successful" or not, when Jesus's body lay in a tomb. Between Good Friday and Easter Sunday is a day that sings of failure. It's known as Holy Saturday, or Easter Eve.

We are living in Holy Saturday times. We do not know what the future holds – in relation to the war in Ukraine and its global repercussions; the current pressures on public and personal finances; the impact of the environmental crisis being seen now.

It is this sense of non-comprehension that speaks most clearly into our experience of failure, or the fear of it at least. It's the place where we don't know what is going to happen, but we fear the worst. It is the pause that we do not yet know is a pause rather than the end. There is sadness in that place, uncertainty, the reality of possible failure, and yet, in that place, God remains.

Lord Jesus, as we live in this time of uncertainty, help us not to fear the future but have faith in your presence now. Amen.

EASTER DAY

"You've
Never Failed"

Easter Day
YOU'VE NEVER FAILED

Read Matthew 28.1-10

> *He is not here, for he has been raised, just as he said.*

Reflection

It's Easter Day. On this joyful day, as we finally stand in the light – rather than the shadow – of the cross, in what sense can we talk about God failing?

The cross must have felt like failure to Jesus – as we reflected on Good Friday. In this way we can say that Jesus experienced failure as we do. He experienced desolation. And yet the cross was very much not failure. If failure is when something doesn't go to plan, the cross was not failure because the cross was God's plan all along.

"You've never failed." Of course, the cross is the answer to all our failures. In the cross Jesus overcame sin and death and hell and all the sin and failure that exists in our world and our hearts. And that means ultimately the end of all failure for everyone.

That is the truth that means that God is able to deal with all our failure, because God alone has never, ever failed.

Alleluia! Christ is risen!

Think back over your journey through this Lent and the work you've done on how we live with failure and sin. What has been the most important insight for you? And how can you take this forward into Easter and beyond?

Lord who is with us every step of the journey, in our despair and our delight, in our failures and our successes, may each moment of our lives be to your glory, and in the name of your Son who died so that failure would never be the end. Amen.

GOING FURTHER

Jesus Christ is at the heart of our vision for the Church of England. Where will a life centred on Christ take you?

We hope you have enjoyed this *Dust and Glory* journey. Here are some ways you might want to travel further in the faith in the days and month ahead:

Join with others in worship and service at your local church. Find thousands of services and events, groups and activities taking place both on site and on line near you via **AChurchNearYou.com**

Sign up for future Church of England reflections. Visit **churchofengland.org** to sign up for future campaigns and resources – including Advent and Christmas reflections. It's free to sign up for emails and you can easily opt out at any time.

Explore God in everyday life with *Everyday Faith*. Everyday Faith provide resources for individuals and churches to help them find and follow God in everyday life – including prayers, reflections and stories. Visit **churchofengland.org/everyday-faith** to find out more.

Take part in *Thy Kingdom Come*. *Thy Kingdom Come* is a global prayer movement inviting Christians to pray during the nine days between Ascension and Pentecost for more people to come to know Jesus Christ. Find out more at **thykingdomcome.global**.